A Writer's Guide to Fame and Fortune

Get the respect you deserve,
the work you want,
and the money you're worth.

AMY LORENTI

Saint Jude Press

ISBN-13: 978-1478391661

DEDICATION

To my son Ryan, for purpose; my sister Rose, for love; my friends Kim and Mark, for support; my Catholic faith, for strength; and my God, for everything.

ACKNOWLEDGMENTS

Without the generosity of Val Sarosky, and the encouragement of Christine M. Hand-Gonzales and Susan Malette, this book may have never been written.

Credits

Cover Design: klearIDEA.com
Cover Photograph: Jane M. Sawyer at TheMorgueFile.com

A Writer's Guide to Fame and Fortune

A Writer's Guide to Fame and Fortune

EXPERT AUTHORS

- Write with purpose and specific goals in mind
- Address the interests, issues and concerns of their readers
- Establish themselves as an expert by writing; standing out as "exceptional" in a world of "average"
- Take control of the publishing process
- Succeed

WHO NEEDS THIS BOOK?

- Business professionals "currently between assignments"

- Expert consultants delegated to accepting projects from anyone who offers a contract

- Seasoned employees who see the best projects go to people younger or less qualified

- Retirees – white collar, blue collar, military; who are not yet ready for full retirement

- Small business owners looking for new and effective ways to market

- Self-employed individuals who find themselves "between projects"

- Lawyers, accountants, and accredited professionals frustrated with networking efforts

- Health care providers struggling to build a practice

- Inventors who need venture capital

- Entrepreneurs impatiently waiting for opportunities to find them

- Administrators of nonprofits desperate for funding

- Graduate students forced to compete in an employer's market

- Every expert who has ever said "Someday, I should write a book"

PREFACE

A Writer's Guide to Fame and Fortune grew from my more than 25 year career as a marketing communications consultant for Fortune 500 companies; along with numerous conversations over recent months with clients, creative freelancers (copywriters, designers, photographers), other consultants, and business professionals – all experts in their respective fields – who are concerned about the state of our economy and its impact on small business. Especially their own.

Even those with the most marketing savvy are not satisfied with their returns from traditional advertising, minimal leads from websites and blogs, and no measurable results from time-consuming social media efforts. They all ask, "What else can I do?"

Don't misunderstand me. These people are extremely smart with years, if not decades, of experience. They know the value of brand building, and keep up with the latest marketing strategies and promotion tactics. Their personal websites offer helpful white papers and relevant reports; with timely posts being added to blog pages on a regular basis. As often as possible, they comment on web sites relevant to their industry, signing off with a link back to their own site. They write articles, put out news releases, and send an occasional newsletter email. Networking events, up-to-date LinkedIn profiles, a business presence on Facebook – they do it all. Some even Tweet. Yet most still have to work hard on new business development, and have not felt comfortable raising their rates in years. If this sounds familiar, it is a fair bet it also sounds familiar to your competition.

On top of that, just about every industry is reeling from tremendous changes as technology and other advances seem to reshape the landscape of business on a daily basis; and in ways no one could have predicted a few short years ago. Businesses and organizations are desperate for knowledgeable people to help them navigate the brave new world in which we all find ourselves.

This spells "opportunity" for independent consultants and service providers, as well as those traditionally employed. Management wants to hear from experts like you, and the sooner the better. However, how do you get their attention?

Become an author.

According to a 2002 survey of 1,006 adult Americans, commissioned by Jenkins Group, Inc. (a Michigan publishing services firm); 81 percent of respondents felt they should write a book. At the time, CEO Jerrold Jenkins said, "6,000,000 Americans have actually written a manuscript – just over 2% of the population – while, based on ISBN numbers assigned, approximately 80,000 books get published each year [*author's note: published in the traditional sense*]." Jenkins added that the number of books annually making it into print is growing, thanks to a boom in independent and self-publishing. "Of course, most people will never get around to committing their thoughts to paper – let alone get them published."

The majority who say they want to write, never do – and of those that do, few get published. Therefore, it is reasonable to place the people who become actual published authors in a small but elite group – the "exceptional." The purpose of this book is to help you become a member that elite group so you can have the chance to experience everything being a published author can mean.

The Amazon Top 10.

As of July 2012, Amazon.com's best reviewed and top selling professional and technical books included:

- *StrengthsFinder 2.0* – Tom Rath
- *Thinking. Fast and Slow* – Daniel Kahneman
- *Good to Great: Why Some Companies Make the Leap...And Others Don't* – Jim Collins
- *The Five Dysfunctions of a Team: A Leadership Fable* – Patrick Lencioni
- *Imagine: How Creativity Works* – Jonah Lehrer
- *Getting to Yes: Negotiating Agreement without Giving In* – Roger Fisher, William L. Ury and Bruce Patton
- *The Tools: Transform Your Problems into Courage, Confidence, and Creativity* – Phil Stultz and Barry Michels

Though covering unique subjects, written by different authors, and either on the list a while or just released; what they all have in common is a Top 10 ranking in a specific nonfiction category on Amazon.com.

What is the point? An Amazon Top 10 book can propel its author to fame and fortune.

Be exceptional.

If one person appears to be as qualified as the next, how can either stand out? An individual rocket scientist in a lab full of equally accredited rocket scientists is "Average;" as in, "The average rocket scientist at NASA follows the XYZ formula..."

Another way to look at it is this: someone high up at NASA says, "I need a rocket scientist," and his or her assistant – without personal bias – beckons to the first person they come across in a white lab coat. However, if the request is, "I need the rocket scientist who wrote that book on green fuels," the assistant will march right past all those Joe Average, Ph.Ds to the one expert who is Exceptional – the published author.

Accepting "average" is like agreeing to defeat before the war even starts. Entrepreneurs, professionals, consultants, and employees who want to attract exceptional opportunities and fair compensation must show they already are *exceptional*.

Perception is rarely reality.

First, and just so we are all clear on this point; you are not "average." The simple fact that you are reading this book, and contemplating writing one yourself, lifts you above 98% of Americans (as per the Jenkins' survey cited earlier). If you require more evidence, look at your clients, customers, or employer; they know you are exceptional, whether they have told you so or not (and most likely, not), or they would not have hired you.

Perception is the culprit here; NOT reality. If you allow yourself to be perceived as "average" and believe that is the way of the world, you lose on two counts: 1) You buy into the false premise that there is nothing special about you, and so accept average work and average compensation; and, 2) you feel compelled to take any offer that crawls through the door.

Not a pretty picture, is it? Then do something different. Do something exceptional. Write a book that will get you the respect you deserve, the work you want, and the money you are worth. The work and dedication it will take to move you and your business from "average" to "exceptional" will seem like nothing compared to the rewards it can bring.

About authorship.

Here are a few benefits expert authors enjoy every day:

Enhanced Credibility

- Respect from clients, customers, employers, colleagues, associates, and employees
- A strong credential (Author)
- Proof of your passion and commitment
- Less need for the hard sell

Raised Status

- Name recognition
- Be known as a subject authority

The Law of Attraction

- Companies and influential individuals come to you
- Prior clients or customers re-engage
- New ventures materialize (speaking engagements, invitations to join various boards, special events and promotions)
- New revenue sources start to flow (book sales, workshops structured around your book)

Increased Rates

- An increase in perceived value allows you to increase your fees; because *expertise is worth more*
- Promotions and raises

Platform Building

- Speaking engagements lead to speech transcripts, videos, and audios on your website
- New experiences lead to material for blog posts
- Media interviews lead to book reviews and feature articles, featured guest spots on radio, television

Most of all, authorship provides the writer with a deep sense of accomplishment; knowing your effort will enrich your life and the lives of those most important to you.

What type of expert are you?

One way to get a glimpse of how your contacts see your expert status is to note who is linking to you on LinkedIn, "friend-ing" you on Facebook, adding you to their circles on Google+, or following you on Twitter. You may find your sphere of influence is wider than you think.

Capture ideas before they disappear.

Writers write. You need something to write in before going any further. Something to record your thoughts and ideas as you work your way through this book. You will also want to keep it with you at all times.

Having a pen and paper handy is the way of writers everywhere. Ideas have a mind of their own. They zoom into your brain – and zoom out in a flash - unless you catch them first. I recommend catching them in some sort of notebook – an "idea notebook."

Examples of things you might want to record in your Idea Notebook would be:

- Items of interest from books (including this one), publications, newspaper articles or online
- Catchy phrases that might make a good book title
- Sound bites from anywhere
- Complaints, issues or concerns voiced by clients, customers, associates and others
- New research sources

So find something to write with, and something to write in – an Idea Notebook.

If you are reading from the print edition of *A Writer's Guide to Fame and Fortune*, you are in luck. It is designed so you can write in it. Simply use the left hand pages to "catch" your ideas.

In Summary

Like anything else in life worth having, writing a book – even about topics you are the most comfortable discussing and explaining – is time consuming and demanding.

Benjamin Franklin said, *"Either write something worth reading or do something worth writing."*

I say, "You already are doing something worth writing about; so start writing."

Catch your ideas by writing on this page.

See Yourself as a Brand

"If the position you seek is worth having, it is worth going after with care. Moreover, if you sell yourself to an employer in a manner that impresses him with your individuality, you probably will receive more money for your services from the very start, than you would if you applied for employment in the usual conventional way."

- FROM THINK AND GROW RICH BY NAPOLEON HILL

Personal branding has received a lot of press over the last few years; creating an entire new industry of coaches, trainers, trust experts, brand analysts, career warfare experts, etc.). For our purposes, we will drop the jargon and trim the rhetoric, and instead think of a personal brand as this: reputation.

Back in 1937 when he wrote *Think and Grow Rich*, the book many still believe positioned him as the definitive expert on how to rise above circumstances to be successful; Napoleon Hill had great respect for those in leadership positions. He believed certain factors were imperative to their becoming leaders, and holding that position with strength. The same factors can be argued to be just as important when building a strong personal brand (or reputation) as an expert.

Think and Grow Rich defines a leader as having a combination of factors.

Catch your ideas by writing on this page.

- *Unwavering courage based upon knowledge of self, and of one's occupation.* No follower wishes to be dominated by a leader who lacks self-confidence and courage. No intelligent follower will be dominated by such a leader very long.

- *Self-control.* The man who cannot control himself, can never control others. Self-control sets a mighty example for one's followers, which the more intelligent will emulate.

- *A keen sense of justice.* Without a sense of fairness and justice, no leader can command and retain the respect of his followers.

- *Definiteness of decision.* The man who wavers in his decisions, shows that he is not sure of himself. He cannot lead others successfully.

- *Definiteness of plans.* The successful leader must plan his work, and work his plan. A leader who moves by guesswork, without practical, definite plans, is comparable to a ship without a rudder. Sooner or later he will land on the rocks.

- *The habit of doing more than paid for.* One of the penalties of leadership is the necessity of willingness, upon the part of the leader, to do more than he requires of his followers.

- *A pleasing personality.* No slovenly, careless person can become a successful leader. Leadership calls for respect. Followers will not respect a leader who does not grade high on all of the factors of a pleasing personality.

- *Sympathy and understanding.* The successful leader must be in sympathy with his followers. Moreover, he must understand them and their problems.

- *Mastery of detail.* Successful leadership calls for mastery of details of the leader's position.

Catch your ideas by writing on this page.

- *Willingness to assume full responsibility.* The successful leader must be willing to assume responsibility for the mistakes and the shortcomings of his followers. If he tries to shift this responsibility, he will not remain the leader. If one of his followers makes a mistake, and shows himself incompetent, the leader must consider that it is he who failed.

- *Cooperation.* The successful leader must understand, and apply the principle of cooperative effort and be able to induce his followers to do the same. Leadership calls for Power, and power calls for Cooperation.

THE EXPERT AUTHOR AS BRAND LEADER

Compare the above factors to an expert author, and a personality profile emerges. The expert author is:

- *Self-confident.* Confidence that originates from proved ability; along with the courage to present a unique point of view; open to differing points of view, yet supported by documented facts and personal experience.

- *Self-controlled.* The ability to set goals, prioritize action steps, and manage schedules.

- *Plays fair.* Judiciously credits sources; never plagiarizing the work of others.

- *Decisive.* Makes well-considered decisions, and acts on them.

- *Prepared.* They plan their work to eliminate guesswork, and – as much as possible – chance.

- *Over delivers.* The tricks of any trade are in the details.

- *Concise.* Communicates clearly.

Catch your ideas by writing on this page.

- *Understanding.* Reflects upon and respects different viewpoints.

- *Detail-oriented.* Knowledgeable in every aspect of their field.

- *Responsible.* Stands behind their work and their word.

- *Collaborative.* When moving outside their realm of expertise, consults and credits other experts in related or complementary fields.

Experts, who earn their stripes through education, experience, and hard work, are – by their very nature – leaders; and leaders are exceptional.

THE VALUE OF AUTHORSHIP

Do you realize expert authors earn thousands of dollars from corporate and special event speaking engagements, are sought out by other experts for collaborative projects, socialize with key decision makers, and reach the top of their game faster than most? Simply because they did what 98% of their contemporaries did not – they wrote and published their book.

Tom, Beverly, and Geoff prove the point:

- Tom Rath: Author of *StrengthFinders 2.0*, and co-author of the #1 New York Times and #1 BusinessWeek bestseller, *How Full Is Your Bucket?* Fee Range: $10,001 to $20,000

- Beverly Kaye: Co-author of *Love Em or Lose Em: Getting Good People to Stay*, which reached the bestseller lists of the Wall Street Journal and Amazon.com, is one of the nation's leading authorities in career issues in the workplace. Fee Range: $20,000 to $30,000

Catch your ideas by writing on this page.

- Geoffrey Moore: Author of *Living on the Fault Line*, Founder, The Chasm Group. Fee Range: $50,000 and above

Yes, the rules of the game have changed, but so have the opportunities available to anyone seeking to stand out in their market or niche. A published book helps certify expertise, attracts revenue, opens up new ventures, and builds a strong personal brand; and it can do it faster than almost anything else we find in our marketing toolbox.

PERCEIVED VALUE LEADS TO REAL MONEY

A Gallup report lists the sales of *StrengthsFinder 2.0* by Tom Rath (SF-2.0) between February of 2007 (when first released) to February of 2009 at one million copies. With an average sales price of $17.67, (the hardcover listed at $24.95, Amazon discounts to $14.39 and digital editions settle around $13.67); over a two-year period, SF-2.0 brought in a minimum of $17,670,000 in cash.

How does the actual compensation affect the perceived value of Mr. Rath's personal brand in comparison to, say, a competent blogger?

10 Steps to Identifying Your Strengths by RG, Business Blogger
Compensation: $0.00 each post
Perceived Brand Value: Average

Compared to:

StrengthsFinder 2.0 by Tom Rath, Author
Compensation: $24,205.47 each and every day for two years
Perceived Brand Value: Exceptional and (with a nod to MasterCard), "Priceless"

Catch your ideas by writing on this page.

Though there are no guarantees that your book – or mine, for that matter – will do as well as the example above, there is no doubt that authorship (backed by a timely and well-written book) is definitely a game changer where perceived value is concerned.

YOUR BRAND IMAGE

Authors are people*, and people are not two-dimensional avatars; though they might use one as a logo if writing science fiction. Depending upon your specialty or field of expertise, you might want to hire a designer to create a logo brand, or create one yourself. For example, a cartoonist might choose to replace his smiling face on a flyleaf with a sketch of him and his dog. At the very least, get a professional photographer to take a series of head shots (you'll want to see them in color and black and white); go to About the Author to see a logo brand using a photograph.

*Occasionally, the "writer" is not a person; reference Uggie, the cute little terrier from the Oscar-winning film, The Artist, whose memoir is due out in the fall of 2012. In that case, hire a photographer for a cover shot of "the dog and his man."

Authors need:

- A professionally photographed head shot, at the minimum, and perhaps one of those "author at home" photographs for the book jacket when your book goes to print
- Distinctive colors, type fonts, illustrations or images that will call to mind your books, website, marketing and promotional materials so they can be recognized as unmistakably yours
- A strong book cover layout, and a clean page design
- A website or landing page to encompass everything

Catch your ideas by writing on this page.

A note about photographers: Most of us have a friend or family member who is the "go to" picture taker during parties and reunions. Ask them for a photo session (and do not forget to give them credit at the beginning of your book if you use their work); however, a professional should handle portraits requiring unusual lighting, or special staging and props.

Visual interpretations of your brand can and do have a tremendous impact on public impression and perception. Make sure these visual aids represent you and your work at its best.

RESOURCES & RECOMMENDATIONS

SEARS PORTRAIT STUDIOS - Sears Portrait Studios do very good work, stand by their service, and will sell you a CD with all the pictures from your photo session, in digital format. See http://www.searsportrait.com

COLOURlovers - A creative community where people from around the world create and share colors, palettes and patterns, discuss latest trends and explore colorful articles. All in the spirit of love." See http://www.colourlovers.com/

DAFONT - Fonts that are available for immediate download, of which the majority are free or available for a small donation. See http://www.dafont.com/

ISTOCKPHOTO - Very high quality stock photography and original vector illustrations. Purchase credits with credit packs or through a subscription plan. Use to download royalty-free images. See http://www.istockphoto.com/

THE MORGUE FILE - Free images for your inspiration, reference and use in your creative work, be it commercial or not! See http://www.morguefile.com/

RECOMMENDED READING - StrengthsFinder 2.0 by Tom Rath is a valuable resource, and can help you zero in on your subject or niche. Available online and in bookstores.

Note: Descriptions are direct from their respective websites.

Catch your ideas by writing on this page.

Think of Yourself as an Author

When we enjoy our work and we are good at it, time flies by, and mountains move. However, when we attempt to do something that does not fall squarely into our comfort zone, very often it is too easy to find excuses and not even begin. Writing is like that; you love it, or you delegate. Notice the word "delegate;" not "hate it" or "avoid writing." Authorship is a game changer – and as read on, you will understand why it is something you should not put off any longer.

"BUT WHAT IF...?"

- I don't have time.
- I can't reveal company secrets.
- I won't find a publisher.
- I can't (or don't like to) write.

Really? Is that all that is standing in your way? Then think about this:

No one ever 'finds' the time to do anything worthwhile; they make the time.

A finished, published book automatically positions its author as exceptional – without revealing trade secrets. Let the competition write their own books; though it's more likely they will end up quoting from yours.

Independent publishers get their work published. Count on it. They take matters into their own hands, and publish their books themselves.

Catch your ideas by writing on this page.

Finally, if you do not like to write, or feel you do not write well, there is an option. Make an audio recording of your book. There are services you can hire afterwards to transcribe your recording into a first draft.

GHOSTWRITERS

You may be someone who simply dreads the idea of parking themselves in front of a computer or a microphone for hours at a time, or just does not enjoy the writing process. If so, consider hiring a professional writer – in this case, a ghostwriter.

Ghostwriters help authors make a plan, create an outline, and set schedules. They can polish a rough first draft, or write the book entirely from notes, research materials, and ongoing conversations with the author. They usually assist with research, and work with the books' editor.

However...

- Hiring a ghostwriter is somewhat expensive. Professionals in the field charge in the neighborhood of $25,000 to $75,000+ to write a book (about $250 per page). Fees can go even higher depending on the author's celebrity, the length of the proposed book, if a traditional book proposal is necessary, and how much research they will be responsible to do.

- Authors will also need to find an editor (or the ghostwriter can recommend one or two) – and pay them over and above the ghostwriting fees.

- Authors sign a binding contract and advance one-third to one-half of the total fee up front; a second payment due after the first draft is completed, and the balance before the final edit.

Catch your ideas by writing on this page.

- Authors pay all expenses incurred during the process relating to preparing the manuscript or doing research (copying, mailing, travel expenses, publication purchases, etc.).

- Authors pay $15,000 to $25,000 extra for the ghostwriter to write a traditional book proposal, including a pitch letter, a chapter list, two or three complete sample chapters, and abstracts for the rest (a paragraph or two on what each chapter will cover). Independent publishers, however, should focus on the chapter list and chapter abstracts.

Well, what is it to be? Will you write your book yourself, or use a professional? Understand that if you really do not have the time or expertise to write your book yourself, and you have enough money to pay for one, hiring a ghostwriter is highly preferable to not writing at all.

ABOUT CO-AUTHORS.

If you and your ghostwriter elect to co-author the book, you will need to consider a number of legal issues such as who will hold the copyright, who will apply for the ISBN, how will costs be divided, who gets how much of the income from book sales, what about speaking engagements, etc. Co-authoring is a complex arrangement, which could be a book all its own and could use the assistance of a good contract lawyer to keep the relationship intact. If you need or want someone to help with the writing, as a first-time author, I would suggest you keep the "ghost" in ghostwriter, and pay his or her fee. You can always try co-authoring on your next book.

Bravo! You have made the decision to move forward with your book. Once it is complete, you will need to get it published, and the quickest way to do that is to publish it yourself.

Catch your ideas by writing on this page.

RESOURCES & RECOMMENDATIONS

DRAGON SPEECH RECOGNITION SOFTWARE - Makes it easier for anyone to use a computer. You talk, and it types. Use your voice to create and edit documents or emails, launch applications, open files, control your mouse, and more. Quickly and easily capture your thoughts and ideas while Dragon helps you get more done faster." See http://www.nuance.com/dragon/index.htm

THE ASSOCIATION OF GHOSTWRITERS - The leading professional organization for ghostwriters of books, articles, speeches, blogs and social media content. Members are experienced and aspiring ghostwriters dedicated to providing high-quality content to their clients, who are executives, organizations, professors, national speakers and other subject-matter experts. For more information, see http://associationofghostwriters.org/

Note: Descriptions are direct from their respective websites.

Catch your ideas by writing on this page.

Grasp the Opportunity

As a graphic designer, I have enjoyed a front-row seat to the evolution of the graphic arts industry over the last few decades. In the early days, I would present design concepts using bright white paper and colored markers. Then artists began preparing boards for commercial printing companies using waxed typeset galleys, and perfect line drawings created on a "personal computer" named for – of all things – a piece of fruit.

Desktop supercomputers and creative software from (primarily) Adobe became so sophisticated they gave computer artists the ability to create three-dimensional, animated illustrations in a few days – when a year or two earlier, the project would have taken weeks if not months.

Today, creative professionals are in seventh heaven accessing technology that transforms the stuff of dreams (or nightmares) into stunning artwork and animation. The same technology gives the first time author the ability to control their destiny, and publish their work themselves.

At the beginning of the revolution, commercial printers, book designers, print houses, publishers, agents, editors and many authors put on a good front. They turned up their noses at the mention of "vanity press" houses or self-publishing outlets. Rightfully ridiculing "get rich quick" hacks and amateur writers who pushed thrown together guides, directories, and reports "deals" like this one:

Catch your ideas by writing on this page.

"... Originally $197, just reduced to $47, however if you buy today, you will receive How To Get Super Rich In 3 Minutes, and all 15 bonus reports for the unheard of price of $19!"

However, what the elite failed to recognize, under all that shoveled dreck, was that these enthusiastic opportunists had found the entrepreneurs' Holy Grail – freedom.

ENTER AMAZON AND COMPANY.

In 2007, Amazon introduced the first Kindle eReader, a device with the capacity to cut the heart out of more than one industry. Barnes & Noble, Sony and others soon followed. Now in its fourth generation, the Kindle Fire and its' Mac and PC friendly applications will give anyone with Internet access the ability to take their entire library of digital books, magazines and other publications with them to read wherever they may be – including the beach (where paperbacks reigned supreme for generations).

Today, even the most hard-nosed publishers and editors from the most prestigious publishing houses agree that independent publishing has proven itself to be what the book reading public wants. They are uncomfortably aware this "upstart" competitor... this Amazon, and others of its ilk ... are successfully wooing even The New York Times most bestselling authors over to the digital world as independents.

I believe this is excellent news for the rest of us.

Catch your ideas by writing on this page.

Publish or (your business might) Perish.

Up until recently, the only avenue open to first-time authors was to convince a traditional publishing house to take a calculated risk, and invest time and money to produce and promote their manuscript. Unfortunately, the publishing process added two or more years to the timeline. Some information would be obsolete before the physical book could reach bookstores.

Not anymore.

This book was written not only to suggest solid reasons for you to start the writing process; but to help you get your manuscript published – in both print and digital format – faster than you ever thought possible.

You provide the expertise and the manuscript, and marketers like Amazon, Barnes & Noble, Smashwords, and others give you – the author – the ability to control your destiny and become an independent publisher.

Note: This book launched through Kindle Direct Publishing as a digital ebook, and became available for sale on Amazon.com within 24 hours.

TRADITIONAL BOOK PUBLISHING

Large publishing houses like Random House, Simon & Schuster, Harper Collins, or John Wiley & Sons are excellent partners to have when you are an established author. The key word is "established," so we will not be going into detail here about how to be published in the traditional sense if you are not – established, that is.

Catch your ideas by writing on this page.

THE BOOK PROPOSAL

A book proposal consists of a letter, a chapter list, two or three finished chapters, and abstracts. When shopping for a publisher, the book proposal is critical to success.

If you are well known for your work (Bill O'Reilly, Melinda Gates, or Colin Powell), or have a Hollywood celebrity status (Will Smith, Jay Leno, or Jamie Lee Curtis), most likely you already have a literary agent under contract to introduce your book proposals to relevant acquisition editors. This keeps the book in play while you work on other projects. If not, you need to find a literary agent; which means you will need to write and submit a complete book proposal to a number of them for consideration. For the expert author with a timely message, this exercise eats up valuable time and resources they may not have; and once submitted, there is no guarantee that an agent will decide they want to represent you.

If you are not well known, but still think you would feel more comfortable working with an agent, you should be able to identify a few who specialize in representing authors like yourself. The Literary Market Place (the LMP) is a guide that provides a complete listing of literary agencies, and are available in most libraries. Another excellent source is The Writer's Market (http://www.TheWritersMarket.com).

BOOK PROPOSAL ELEMENTS

1. The Pitch Letter, including a detailed Author Platform
2. A Chapter List
3. Two or Three Sample Chapters
4. Chapter Abstracts

Catch your ideas by writing on this page.

ABOUT LITERARY AGENTS

Literary agents usually have relationships with acquisition editors in a number of publishing houses – large and small. They will know right away who to contact with your book proposal. If your agent is well known and respected, the proposal rises to the top of the editor's review pile. Another benefit of having an agent is that they will constantly be on the lookout for new opportunities for you. Last – but not by any means least – an experienced literary agent knows the publishing business inside and out. They know what to negotiate and what to watch out for within the fine print of a publishing contract so you – the author – will end up with the best terms.

Sounds great, doesn't it? It is, until it comes to money. Agents charge for their knowledge and access – as they should; they are experts, after all. However, an author can fork over more than 15% of their royalty check to their literary agent. Forever.

So, let us say you are not already a bestselling author in your genre. Nor are you a well-known celebrity. You do not personally know anyone at a large publishing house (at least not anyone that has "acquisitions editor" in their title), and you do not have the time or patience required to find and retain a literary agent. Whom do you go to for help?

Yourself.

Catch your ideas by writing on this page.

THE DIGITAL REVOLUTION AND SELF PUBLISHING

When we look at where the publishing industry has been and where it seems to be going, an "ah ha" moment occurs.

According to the December 2011 issue of *TechJournal*, "Ereader growth will triple ebook revenue by 2016... We buy more books than anyone we know and *we have shifted to buying ebooks when possible, particularly for new releases* [italics by author]."

In the same article, Juniper Research reported "Continued strong growth in the dedicated eReader market, allied to an upsurge in usage across tablet devices, will push annual revenues from ebooks delivered to portable devices to $9.7 billion by 2016... up from $3.2 billion (in 2011)."

In late March of 2012, VentureBeat.com reported:

"Ebooks [purchased by adults] are also showing huge growth, surging from 66.6 million ebooks sold in January 2011 to 99.5 million sold in January 2012."

"Adult ebooks are set to overtake adult paperbacks as the highest volume product for publishers in America. This past January, paperbacks outsold ebooks by less than 6 million units; *if ebook market growth continues, it will have far outpaced paperbacks to become the number-one category for U.S. publishers.*"

Ebook readers (anything that can read a digital book) include the iPhone, iPod, and iPad devices from Apple; Android phones and other Smartphones; tablets; PC and Mac computers used as eReaders after downloading free eReader software.

Not only is the revolution here, it is winning the war.

Catch your ideas by writing on this page.

THE EXPERT AUTHOR AND THE NEED FOR SPEED

As an independent publisher, there are three ways to go:

1. *Digital publishing.* The fastest way to publish a book like this one is to launch it as a digital eBook and follow up with a print edition. Digital eBooks get in front of an audience of many thousands (if not millions) of readers within hours of being uploaded to digital publishers like Kindle Direct Publishing (Amazon) or PubIt! (Barnes & Noble).

2. *Print on demand (POD).* A POD book can be available for sale within a few months – depending upon the expertise of the person submitting the compiled manuscript for publication. The print publisher holds your title, takes orders, prints one book or many, and ships to the purchaser. You can pay anywhere from low or no money to a few thousand dollars for a POD publisher to set up your book to do this. It depends upon which print on demand printer you go with and the percentage of the cut they take (no percentage, high prep costs; high percentage, low or no prep costs).

3. *Self-publishing printers.* Speakers, teachers, and other experts may need dozens to hundreds of copies of their book during conferences, in classrooms or at customer meetings. These authors have the option of using their POD (print on demand) printer – especially if the deadline is close; however, the price per book could be very high. If you believe you will have the need for a large number of copies of your book, you will find most self-publishing houses offer packages specializing in high volume discounts.

Catch your ideas by writing on this page.

Expert authors interested in getting their books out to the public quickly should opt for number one; establish themselves as an independent publisher, and launch their book digitally. To determine which publisher is right for you, check the resources at the end of this section. *A Writer's Guide to Fame and Fortune* launched with Kindle Direct Publishing for the Amazon Kindle Store, and is now in print. Amazon supports this approach:

"Many authors and publishers using KDP to publish their books on Kindle also have a physical edition published through CreateSpace or another publishing house.

Linking these various formats to one another in the Amazon catalog provides the ideal browsing experience for customers."

ABOUT ISBN NUMBERS

An ISBN number is a unique, internationally utilized code assigned to all printed books for the purposes of identification and inventory control. www.isbn.org is the only authorized United States ISBN number distributor.

If you plan to release your book in digital format only, you will not require an ISBN number (and save yourself around $125). Retailers like Amazon and Barnes & Noble assign a sales tracking code for your book as an inventory number, so an ISBN number would appear to be redundant.

However, the ISBN number does lock you in as the owner of the work. It is like assigning a driver's license or social security number to individual books. Therefore, if you plan to publish your book as a hardcover or paperback in the future, you will need ISBN numbers; one for the hardcover edition and one for the paperback. When future editions of your book come out, they also will need a separate ISBN number.

Catch your ideas by writing on this page.

RESOURCES & RECOMMENDATIONS

KINDLE DIRECT PUBLISHING - With Kindle Direct Publishing (KDP) you can self-publish your books on the Amazon Kindle Store. It's free, fast, and easy. Books self-published through KDP can participate in the 70% royalty program and are available for purchase on Kindle devices and Kindle apps for iPad, iPhone, iPod touch, PC, Mac, BlackBerry, and Android-based devices. With KDP, you can self-publish books in many languages – including English, German, French, Spanish, Portuguese, and Italian – and specify pricing in US Dollars, Pounds Sterling, and Euros. You will also find useful information on the active community forum. See https://kdp.amazon.com/self-publishing/signin

PUBIT! BY BARNES & NOBLE - PubIt! is an online, self-service Web portal where independent publishers and authors can upload their eBooks and make them available for sale through the Barnes & Noble eBookstore. This easy-to-use distribution platform offers qualified users the expanded distribution, visibility, and protection that only Barnes & Noble can offer. EBooks, essays, articles, poems, and short stories sold through the Barnes & Noble eBookstore are available for sale on BN.com, NOOK eBook Readers, and our free NOOK eReading software for iPad, iPhone/iPod touch, Mac, Android, PC, etc. See http://www.pubit.barnesandnoble.com

SMASHWORDS.COM – Smashwords.com distributes to Apple's iBookstore, Barnes & Noble, Sony Reader Store, Kobo, the Diesel eBook Store, Baker & Taylor's Blio and Axis360 (libraries) and more. See http://www.smashwords.com/

THE LITERARY MARKET PLACE - See your local library for access.

AGENT QUERY - A database of literary agents.
http://www.agentquery.com/default.aspx

THE WRITERS' MARKET - See http://www.writersmarket.com/

ISBN NUMBERS - Authorized U.S. Distributor: http://www.isbn.org

Note: Descriptions are direct from their respective websites.

Catch your ideas by writing on this page.

STEP 5

Look at the Big Picture

- The sum total of your talents, experience, and expertise is what makes you an expert. This automatically makes you unique. Not average. Take what makes you unique and – through authorship – become exceptional.

- Authorship comes with great benefits. Keep them in mind every time you think the work involved might be too much.

- You – the writer, the one-of-a-kind you – are a brand; just like Nike, Coke, IBM, and Chick-Fil-A. Brands have real value (money, status, power).

- The writing process is a mental decision (the thought) followed by action (actual writing). Write your book yourself, or hire someone else to write it for you, but write it.

- Advances in technology and brilliant marketers have given writers a huge gift – the ability to take our destiny into our own hands, and not depend upon the agendas, expectations, or timetables of literary agents or traditional book publishers. We still want them around, of course; once a digital eBook gets their attention, a publishing contract can offer resources a first-time author can only dream about; in the meantime, no problem. You just publish your book yourself.

- Choose to launch your book in digital format with a reputable eBook marketer. It is the fastest way to get your book to the marketplace.

Catch your ideas by writing on this page.

$\mathcal{P}$repare to $\mathcal{W}$rite

GOAL SETTING

Every how-to and self-help advocate stresses the importance of setting goals for a new project. Becoming an expert author is all about setting goals and making a plan to reach them. When you have a clear vision of where you want to end up when your book is finished; that vision will be what keeps you going when the writing gets hard; and, trust me, it will get hard – but the result will be well worth the effort.

WRITE WITH PURPOSE

Link your goals to your dreams. Think about what you want to happen as though it already has happened. For example, "I want to be booked solid as a corporate speaker."

State your goal like this, "My speaking schedule is packed through to the end of next year."

Close your eyes and visualize yourself sitting down to write, finishing your book, submitting it for publication, and experiencing your goal. See your book as one of Amazon's Top 10 in your category. You can do this exercise in less than a minute – though take as long as you need in order to feel the experience is real.

And remember: *"A goal is a dream with a deadline."*

- NAPOLEON HILL

-

Catch your ideas by writing on this page.

The use of goal linking – associating what you want as a done deal (speaking engagements) directly to an action you do (write a book), is white magic. I am not taking a position on either side of the "affirmations" fence; I am simply recommending you suspend disbelief (we do it every day when in front of a TV or in a movie theater), and believe what you are "seeing." It is much easier to give something your best because you already believe the outcome is a given.

RIGHT BRAIN, LEFT BRAIN

Fiction writers love surprises. As storytellers who rely on creativity, subjective feeling, and intuition to lead their blindfolded imagination from first scene to the final chapter, they stumble across a number of revelations along the way. Right-brain activities invite surprises. Frequently, the writer asks, 'What if...?,' and then follows the question to its unexpected answer which may not be revealed until the story ends. The best works of fiction are full of twists and turns that can stun the senses – as they are meant to do.

Not so much with nonfiction writing, which uses left-brain skills of logic, analysis, sequence, and objective reasoning to examine and explain a subject, in whole or in part.

Both fiction and nonfiction authors should know who they are writing to (market), and what their market wants to read about (subject). With more of a sense of purpose than of inspiration, the nonfiction writer sets out to discuss his or her subject using structure and a progression of facts, figures, and supporting documentation, among other things, to educate, inform, or convince. Satisfaction comes from communicating clearly and concisely. What readers do with the information afterward is up to them. The writer has done their job.

Catch your ideas by writing on this page.

STEP 7

Plan Your Book

Your mission must be to seek out and address the interests, issues, and concerns of your reader. To do this, you need to know what exactly they are – and for that, you need a plan.

A well-thought out book plan saves time, focuses thinking, assures that important information is not left out, and divides what could be a huge undertaking into manageable segments. Plan your work, and work your plan – the best advice an aspiring author can ever receive. Before you will be able to do that, however, you need to ask the right questions.

THE IDEA NOTEBOOK

Use this book, or get a lined notebook or pad of paper, and answer the following questions as completely as you can. Do not worry about those you may not be able to answer right away. As you move through the steps in this book, you will come up with the answers.

Note: If one question or an answer leads to other questions, write them down and answer them as well. This is stream of consciousness thinking exercise; you will be calling on your years of experience and expertise to help you answer and ask questions that, when you are finished, will help you construct a rock solid book plan.

On the next pages are questions – in no particular order – to get the ball rolling. We have added space under each for your answers, though you may want to use your idea notebook instead.

How do I define my market?

What do I want from them?

What do I want them to remember after reading my book?

What should they do next?

What am I going to write about?

Which issues, concerns, problems, or advances in my industry are hot right now?

Who suffers the most impact? Why?

What do I bring to the table that no one else does?

Is my subject timely?

Who is my competition?

Who else writes about these subjects?

Are these authors well regarded, and credible?

Where will I find the time to write?

What will it take to write a book that could really add something to the discussion?

Will there be a lot of research required? Where will I find answers to questions outside of my field?

What topics need to be part of individual chapters?

Which sub-topics should come under each?

Do I have a title and subtitle?

Do they check out in Google as having low competition; are they highly searched keywords or phrases?

Do they show up in Amazon's search box?

What should I include as part of my author biography?

What are my credentials?

What makes me the right person to write this book?

What makes up a successful book cover design, and where do I get one if I am not a designer?

Should I use a photograph, illustration or just a simple typeface?

How will I publish my book?

Is Kindle enough; what about using NOOK and the others?

How will I market this book?

What marketing tactics are already in place that can work for me? Do I have a platform?

What comes next?

How do I even start?

[Use the space below for additional questions that came to mind while doing this exercise.]

Now that you have it all written down, you have a reference to go back to as we work through the next chapters, tackling one big question at a time.

RESOURCES & RECOMMENDATIONS

GOOGLE KEYWORD - See http://adwords.google.com

AMAZON SEARCH - See http://www.amazon.com

Catch your ideas by writing on this page.

Identify Your Ideal Market

A child wants candy. The child will hug any member of her family who gives her candy. Who will trade candy for hugs?

Mom? You would think so. However, even though she likes hugs very much, she would rather have a child with healthy teeth. The little girl could hug her mother all day long and, though it would please her, Mom would not hand over the candy.

Mom is in the marketplace – but she is not the little girl's ideal market.

So who will trade candy for hugs?

Grandmother? Bingo. Princess gives Grandma a big hug, and she gets the candy.

Grandma is her ideal market – the target market – because she wants to experience the child's love.

In the last step, you answered a number of questions. What answers did you give to these?

- How would I define my ideal reader – my market?
- What does my ideal reader want that only I can give them?
- What do they need (or want) from me?

Your answers most likely identified your ideal market. Target your writing to them.

Catch your ideas by writing on this page.

A goal linking exercise.

"What do I want to be able to say after my book is published?"

EXAMPLES

1. *PODIATRIST "I now have so many patients; I have to add another podiatrist and two nurses to my staff."*

2. *COLLEGE ADMISSIONS COUNSELOR "Online sales of college admissions consulting packages are skyrocketing."*

3. *AUTHOR "Random House just called with an offer to buy the publishing rights to A Writer's Guide to Fame and Fortune."*

Who could make that happen? Who should be the author's target market or ideal reader?

1. The podiatrist's ideal readers should include people with foot problems, referring physicians and surgeons, podiatry associations, current and prospective patients, media covering the health beat, etc.

2. The college admissions consultant ideal readers should include parents, students, high school teachers, administrators, counselors, parent groups, home school associations, past and current clients, etc.

3. A Writer's Guide to Fame and Fortune ideal readers should include small business owners, independent health practitioners, entrepreneurs, business professionals, the self-employed, inventors, any and all aspiring nonfiction authors; the author's email, Google+, LinkedIn, Facebook and Twitter contacts; and, of course, the senior acquisitions editor at RH.

Catch your ideas by writing on this page.

You know what you want, and you have identified the target market that can help you get it. That is all you need to know, right? Not quite.

The real question: "What's in it for me?"

Your only answer: "Solutions to your problems."

Before you can provide solutions, you need to identify your ideal readers' problems. Ask questions. What do they want to know about? What are their interests? What is most important to them? Who is important to them? Whom do they look to for advice or information if it is not you? Why should it be you?

Take the first example involving the podiatrist.

- THE AUHOR'S GOAL - "I now have so many patients, I have to add another podiatrist, and two nurses to my staff."

- THE AUTHOR'S IDEAL READER - The doctor's current and prospective patients

- THE IDEAL READER'S PROBLEM - Foot pain that crops up at all hours of the day and night

- WHAT THE IDEAL READER REALLY WANTS - To be pain free, of course; but short of that, they want to be able to take care of the pain themselves as much as possible.

- THE SOLUTION THE PODIATRIST AUTHOR PROVIDES - A complete list of foot symptoms and their effect on overall health with solutions for each; listing natural products and alternative treatments sufferers can try before hobbling off to a podiatrist and paying for a specialist.

Catch your ideas by writing on this page.

What will our expert podiatrist author get in return? Ongoing referrals and terrific word of mouth leading to so many patients, he has to add another podiatrist and two nurses to his staff.

RESOURCES & RECOMMENDATIONS

LinkedIn – See http://www.linkedin.com to set up a free account

Facebook – See http://www.facebook.com to set up a free account

Google+ – See https://plus.google.com/ to set up a free account

Twitter – See http://www.twitter.com to set up a free account

Catch your ideas by writing on this page.

STEP 9

Decide on a Subject

WHAT TO WRITE ABOUT

Ask yourself, "Which issues, concerns, problems, or advances in my industry are hot buttons for my ideal reader?" In the simplest sense, write about that.

WRITING IS A BUSINESS

At the end of the day, unless you are privileged or independently wealthy, nonfiction writing is a business. And like any other, the more customers you attract the more sales you make; the more reader groups you identify, the more you can expect from book sales, consulting offers and speaking engagements.

Before writing a word, be reasonably certain there is enough of a market or audience for the book you want to write. Will enough people be interested in your subject and your unique perspective to click "BUY NOW" and make the considerable effort of researching, writing, and promoting your book worthwhile? This is where you put in time and effort to choose your subject because – no matter how enthusiastic you may be about something – you want to be certain your readers are, too.

The Jenkins' survey mentioned earlier found 28% of respondants said they would write a self-help/do-it-yourself book, 27% a work of fiction, 27% general nonfiction (history, biography, etc.); and 20% some other type (cookbook, picture book, etc.). Mr. Jenkins said, "The bulk of prospective authors sees themselves writing some form of non-fiction, be it a biography, self-help, do-it-yourself, or cookbook." Know what this tells me about these would be writers – and should tell you?

Catch your ideas by writing on this page.

- 28% of readers are interested in learning how to do things themselves
- 27% of readers enjoy reading stories
- 27% of readers are fascinated by historical figures and events
- 20% of readers like to cook, look at pictures – or both

You should be able to find dozens of "how to" subjects you might address that would appeal to the first group alone.

THE IDEAL READER

A Fable for Aspiring Authors

An expert on the reproductive life of the American cockroach knows everything about that immortal of the insect world. It does not matter if you or I have the same (or any) interest in this subject. What does matter – for making my point and if our expert plans on earning an income while pursuing her passion – is whether there are others who share her enthusiasm; and if so, will they pay to know what she knows.

Using online booksellers like Amazon, Barnes and Noble, Textbooks.com, and CampusBooks.com she searches for her subject and sees few nonfiction books (if any) about cockroach reproduction. She perceives this as good news, but that is not the case. If no one is writing about a specific subject, most likely that is because no one else is interested in reading about it.

Our expert does a Google search for "cockroach reproduction" and gets 331,000 hits (which I just did and that's what came up), which tells her there are a number of other experts like herself providing information on her subject (but as her first exercise revealed, they are not writing books about it).

Catch your ideas by writing on this page.

Next, she uses Google's keyword tool and finds the key word phrase "cockroach reproduction" nets 1,900 monthly searches by people who are potentially in her target market; however, "how to get rid of cockroaches" nets 40,500. These are actual results, with related search terms adding thousands more to the 40,500.

Who should our cockroach expert want to reach with her book? Though "Cockroach Reproduction, the Real Story" might be a neat hook for a few readers, interest is sparse. However, "Get Rid of Cockroaches Naturally – A Franchise Owner's Guide to an A+ Rating with Customers and the Department of Health" could sell thousands of books, garner a celebrity-making interview on NPR, attract the interest of hundreds of thousands of restaurant franchise owners who want to retain our expert's natural bug-ridding services, and get her booked to speak (first class, all expenses paid) at their next soiree in New York City.

SUBJECT HUNTING

1. Look around your office and collect every book or publication you have read, or plan to read and sort them into piles according to subject matter.

2. Turn on your computer and check your browser history and bookmarks; then do the same thing you did with your books and magazines. You can sort URLs into subject folders or print the pages out and add them to the appropriate piles.

3. Check file cabinets and piles of papers. Retrieve articles you have written (published, submitted or in progress), as well as those you kept that are written by others. If printed, physically add them to the subject piles. If in digital format, drag them to subject folders.

Catch your ideas by writing on this page.

4. If you have a blog, write down your categories, tags, and topics.

5. Whom do you "fan" on Facebook, put in "circles" on Google+, or "follow" on Twitter? While you are in the social media realm, note who your fans are, who has you in circles, and who follows you. This will give you ideas about the type of "expert" these people think you are.

6. Now, write down the names you assigned your subject piles and folders. Rank them according to how much information or good "stuff" is in each, or that you refer to the most, or both. The top two or three on that list represent the subjects you:
   a. Know the most about, and
   b. Are most interested in

By taking an objective look at what you read or access on a regular basis, enjoy learning about, or simply where your brain likes to spend its' time, you should get a clear idea which subjects you could write about intelligently, with commitment, and with passion. It also tells you that there are likely to be other people interested in the exact same subject matter, because you will discover that there are already a number of books, periodicals and websites covering those topics.

When I first completed The Subject Hunt, it was clear that my interests involved marketing and sales promotion for the self-employed and small business owner; taking advantage of the new opportunities available online for those markets; and – frankly – finding shortcuts to make them pay off.

Try it. There is a good chance you will find the perfect subject right in front of you.

Catch your ideas by writing on this page.

SUBJECTS, SUBJECTS, EVERYWHERE

Finding things to write about is easy. Just look around you. But choosing the subject your ideal reader wants to read about - from those subjects identified in the "hunt" - takes added effort.

- Use Google.com and Bing.com to see how many other people are writing about your subject ideas

- Visit a bookstore and physically browse its shelves for titles and subjects that catch your attention in your niche (for example: Science / Earth Science / Insects / Cockroach)

- Use the Google Keyword Tools to see how many people search using the words and phrases that relate to your subject matter

- Think about your subject and different ways to present it

START PLANNING YOUR NEXT BOOK

I realize you may not have written word one of your first book yet, let alone started thinking about your next one; but as you read through the process in *A Writer's Guide to Fame and Fortune*, ideas will begin popping into your head at the oddest moments. You don't want to lose these elusive gems. I recommend capturing them here or in your Idea Notebook.

RESOURCES & RECOMMENDATIONS

Google.com – See http://www.google.com

Bing.com – See http://www.bing.com

Google Keyword Tool – See http://adwords.google.com

Amazon Search Box – See http://www.amazon.com

TrendsMap.com – See http://trendsmap.com/

Catch your ideas by writing on this page.

Meet the Competition

OTHER AUTHORS, OTHER BOOKS

Most likely you are not the only expert out there writing about your topic, so it is smart to know who your book will be sharing cyber shelf space with (and later, bookstore and library shelf space). The idea is not to "best" these authors, who may well become friends, colleagues, or collaborators in the future, but to complement or build on their good work and identify your books' place among them.

It also helps to understand what is going on in your subject area in general. The New York Times *Topics*, Amazon.com's *Bestselling Books*, and BarnesandNoble.com *Bestseller Books* are good resources to use for reviewing other titles in your niche. Buy those books. Read them. Then write up a short analysis to include their titles, what topics they cover, and how your book compares.

Select books most similar to what you plan to write about, and which targets a similar market or markets. Does your book offer new information not available anywhere else? Does it expose inaccuracies or deceptions? Does your research agree or disagree? Maybe your book simply provides a unique point of view – yours.

In your Idea Notebook, be sure to put down any ideas you have that can add to or enhance these already successful books. Your mission is to share in their success by building on it.

Catch your ideas by writing on this page.

CULTIVATE YOUR COMPETITION

You've identified your competition, now get to know them. Buy their books, and read them. Then when your book goes live on Kindle, go back and comment in a positive way, and include a link back to your book. This will do two things:

1. Add a back link to your book from an already established book, and

2. Increase the chance to have your book on Amazon's "Customers who bought this item also bought..."

RESOURCES & RECOMMENDATIONS

The New York Times Topics – See http://nyti.ms/Qa5ROO

Amazon.com/Bestselling Books – See http://amzn.to/QabiwE

BarnesandNoble.com/Bestseller Books – See http://bit.ly/QabEDr

Catch your ideas by writing on this page.

Take Stock

Your market is an open book; you know who you will need to attract in order to get to your goals. You know what these ideal readers want in return, and your book will give it to them.

Your subject matter is clear, you have identified where your own passions lie, and you know what unique input you can add to the discussion.

Research supports there is an audience for your subject.

Competitive authors are future friends and colleagues as far as you should be concerned, because your book plan includes complementing and building upon their hard work – not copying it.

It is time to get serious about writing.

Catch your ideas by writing on this page.

Get Serious about Writing

Find a private place to work. Stack up your research materials, relevant files, and documents on the desk or a nearby table. Check that the Internet connection to your laptop or computer is working. Perhaps get a glass of cool water to have on hand. Don't forget to use the bathroom. Yes; now you are ready to write.

Get ready, get set...**Go!**

Anything happening?

No?! Nothing?

Why not? You've set your goals; know your ideal reader and what you are going to write about; and you aren't worried about the competition. Did your mind just go blank? Maybe you are second guessing your decision to write a book; still not convinced you have what it takes. Worried about what others will think or say when they hear about your project? Or has some other emotional weasel pinned your creative mind down in a choke hold? Without meaning to sound insensitive, the best advice I can give is this: shake the weasel off and write anyway.

Not that you need reminding, but here goes; the primary reason to do what needs doing and write a book is to help your business or career succeed. Only you can do this. The decision you make to establish yourself as an expert should be a business decision – not a personal one. Think of this as a make-or-break project for your most important client; and get to work.

Catch your ideas by writing on this page.

I firmly believe writer's block – for lack of a better term – is self inflicted and mired in emotion, not fact. Too many worthwhile projects have stuttered to a halt because of self doubt. The best thing to do is to acknowledge the feeling, soldier through it, and write anyway.

SET A SCHEDULE AND STICK TO IT

At the beginning of each week, schedule in at least an hour each day to write. Use any calendar you are comfortable with; a bound appointment book or an app on your iPhone – the important thing is that you set aside enough time for writing. Some think an hour a day is enough. I find a minimum of two hours a day is necessary to see progress. If you are really serious about getting your book completed and published, double or triple the time. I usually work in two to three hour blocks, twice a day, every day.

Get up an hour early to write. Until your book is finished, cut everything that is not absolutely essential or important. Date night with your spouse, attending the kid's ball games, class plays and dance recitals are important. Poker night with the boys or girl's night out? Not important (until you celebrate when your book is finished).

At the end of the day, make a note of what you worked on and list the top two or three tasks you would like to get done during the next day's scheduled session(s). This keeps you focused and on track to meet your publication date.

The process need not be complicated. The following example is what a work schedule entry on your calendar, spreadsheet, or in your Idea Notebook might look like:

Catch your ideas by writing on this page.

Today: Write from 9 until 10:30 am, and 2 until 3:00 pm; Finish the chapter outline

Tomorrow: Begin chapter abstracts, schedule photo session for a formal head shot

LEARN HOW TO SAY "NO"

Someone outside your family – not a current client or customer – asks a favor. "Now, if possible. Right now."

You are in the middle of writing your book. What do you do? Before you commit to adding one other activity or project to your plate, think about your cat (or your neighbor's cat) and what it would say if it could talk.

"What's in it for me?"

Of course, if you want to keep the relationship, don't actually say that out loud; but think about what this individual is really asking you to do. They want you to stop writing. They want you to put aside one of the most important things you can do for yourself and your business, and help them. Their request is actually this: "Ignore your goals. Focus on mine. I come first. You can wait."

Think of Whiskers, smile nicely, and say, *"Sorry, I'm booked."*

ASK FOR HELP WHEN AND WHERE YOU NEED IT

Perhaps you are more creative than technical; more right brain than left. You might want to ask a friendly accountant or engineer to compile necessary statistics, tables or graphs for you; crediting them for their contribution. More technical than creative; left brain than right? Ask a designer to create a professional book cover, and credit them.

Catch your ideas by writing on this page.

When you credit your contributors, they will happily recommend your book to their circle of influence because they were a part of it. A win/win situation all around.

JUMP START THE WRITING PROCESS

The antidote for writer's block is encouragement.

You may have more of your book completed or in draft form than you think. Every proposal written, presentation or speech given, article published, manuscript started, course taught, research conducted, references cited, or blog post you have written on your subject could find a place in your book. Sort them according to topic and importance, then see what can be used.

RESOURCES & RECOMMENDATIONS

An online or old school calendar.

Your Idea Notebook.

Your files and folders of subject materials.

The results of your Subject Hunt.

Catch your ideas by writing on this page.

Write the Chapter Outline

WHY THE TABLE OF CONTENTS COMES FIRST

When you plan the flow of topic to topic, chapter to chapter, it becomes makes easier to write the content. The chapter outline becomes a road map that stops at all the interesting places along the way from Introduction to In Summary, and becomes the book's Table of Contents. As an example, this is an excerpt from the chapter outline of *A Writer's Guide to Fame and Fortune*; early on in the process. Though it doesn't match the final table of contents word for word, it helped keep the writing on track. A chapter outline should be able to stand alone as a representation of what the book is about.

> *Introduction.*
> */ Join the elite.*
> */ Be exceptional.*
> *The big picture.*
> *You – the Brand.*
> */ Perceived value = real dollars.*
> *You – the Writer.*
> */ Ghostwriters.*
> */ Authorship*

Craft the chapter outline; it will become your table of contents (TOC). A well thought out TOC can make all the difference on whether a reader decides to "Buy Now with 1-Click" or move on to another authors' book; and we certainly don't want that.

Catch your ideas by writing on this page.

ORGANIZE THE FLOW OF INFORMATION

1. Start with those piles you used to determine what you were going to write about, and add the draft materials you pulled together to jump start the writing process in the last chapter.

2. Put them in subject categories or topics and write those categories on 3" x 5" cards. Then start sorting, look for common denominators, and stack accordingly. Pretty soon you will see a coming together of facts and ideas.

3. Some categories (chapter titles or headings) will be rich with information and broken into sub-categories (subheads), others may have a line or two written on a napkin which means more thought and research might be needed.

As you add to and rearrange the 3 x 5 cards, a pattern will begin to emerge. Plug the holes, organize the flow of information – and soon a Table of Contents, complete with titles, headings and subheads will emerge. Type it up and use it as your outline for the book. In this way, as you are writing, one idea will lead to the next in natural order.

WRITE CHAPTER SUMMARIES

The chapter abstract summarizes what a chapter will be about. You should write one for each chapter or sub chapter in your table of contents. They can be as short as a few sentences or up to one or two paragraphs.

This exercise can give you enough information to estimate book length and set the writing schedule you began in the above section. For instance, if you can schedule enough time each day to write 750 to 1000 words, and you write five days a week, you could write the first draft of a 50,000 word book in seven to ten weeks.

Catch your ideas by writing on this page.

Write the First Draft

An editor friend of mine, who is also a prolific writer with six novels under his belt, says this about first drafts: *"Just write. Don't edit, don't backspace, don't stop. Let the words flow. Start at the beginning and end at – well, the end."* It works for him; he writes fiction. The nonfiction author does better with a bit more structure.

What I did to write this book was to start fast, level out, then slow down until my outline was fleshed out to a first draft and ready to edit. This technique allowed me to really move the writing process along.

The Sprint - Use your chapter outline as a guide, and write as much as possible within the time you have scheduled that day so to get your initial thoughts and main points briefly covered. Don't correct spelling, don't go back and edit – not now. However; if you are ready to fully cover a topic, do so. When the writing is flowing, you don't want to stop it to follow an exercise – one in this book or any other.

The Jog - Now go chapter by chapter and add in detail; headings, subheads, examples, case studies, quotes, supporting illustrations, etc. to check that the flow of information makes sense.

The Stretch - Fine-tune the table of contents: headings, chapter titles, sub-titles etc. Start adding solid information. Use your research, the Internet, etc., and put in everything you think needs to be under the relevant category in your table of contents. There will be time to tighten the whole thing up in the editing process. Take out extraneous words you come across, check the flow of information, use highly searched keyword phrases whenever possible, and lightly edit as you go.

Catch your ideas by writing on this page.

PAY ATTENTION TO TECHNIQUE

Nonfiction writing is a craft unto itself. Here are a few rules to keep in mind as you write.

- Use a compelling voice.
- Data and detail information should be introduced a little at a time, so as not to overwhelm the reader.
- Be clear and concise.
- Remember that proper grammar, spelling and punctuation count.
- Write simply; choose to be understood over impressing the reader with your eloquence.
- Avoid jargon, acronyms, cliches, and texting abbreviations.

Catch your ideas by writing on this page.

STEP 15

Edit for the Critics in Your Life

I may be too late, but this seems like the place to beg forgiveness for any misspellings, typos, grammatical errors, or misused words that you may find in this book. Sometimes, no matter how careful one is, or how many people proofread your work, those critters show up anyway. Mea culpa, mihi ignoscas. – AL

People can be tough. Teachers, coaches, bosses, clients, customers, colleagues, spouses, children, neighbors, and – of course – in-laws. They are fast to call us out for real or imagined mistakes. Think about them. Who stands out as the most "helpful"? Think of the person who is always first to say "Too bad, you just missed that putt," and only too happy to instruct you on what they believe you need to do in order to improve your short game. These kind souls are always looking out for you, aren't they?

Pull out a red pen, write that jokers' name on it with a permanent marker, and use it to edit. Use it a lot. The goal here is to render them *speechless*.

HOW DOES IT SOUND?

Even if you have used spelling and grammar checking programs and your manuscript looks clean, read what you have written – but read it OUT LOUD. You can do this yourself or use a software application that is capable of reading your words back to you.

Catch your ideas by writing on this page.

Reading aloud is a good way to check that your writing is "in your voice." Rewrite anything that sounds choppy, awkward, or simply not like you. I recommend you do as much of this as you can in a single sitting; though for longer manuscripts, that is not always possible. I find this works well to catch cliches, double words, misspellings, and grammar nightmares.

"I LIKE THE WAY THIS GUY WRITES!"

If you answer "no" to any of these questions, you could lose readers:

- Is your subject timely, unique and presented in a logical fashion?
- Is the information you are presenting interesting and factual?
- Does the subject appeal to a wide enough audience?
- Is it well-written, with proper spelling, grammar and sentence structure?
- Does it avoid scientific or technical terminology that the average reader might not understand?
- Does it contain jargon or slang expressions that might date the work?
- Is the writing easy to understand?
- Is the material well-organized?
- Is the title descriptive and the cover art attention getting?
- Is the presentation appealing and professional-looking?

Catch your ideas by writing on this page.

DEATH BY SPELL CHECK

You should know not to place your trust in built-in spelling and grammar tools. Excellent, and reasonably priced software applications are released almost every day; do a search, review what's available and download one or two to check your work. Many are free for individual use.

PLAYING FAIR

Do not copy and paste. If you need something written by someone else to make your point – use quotes and credit the writer. Do not plagiarize. It's dishonest. It suggests a defective character. Copying someone's work and passing it off as your own is just wrong. Don't do it.

RESOURCES & RECOMMENDATIONS

Online Dictionary – Dictionary.com (free)

Online Thesaurus – Thesaurus.com (free)

Online Grammar Checker – Grammarly.com (free and paid versions)

AutoCrit.com - http://autocrit.com/ - The AutoCrit Editing Wizard is an instant book editor. With the click of a button it shows you the problems in your manuscript. (Subscription service) – from the AutoCrit.com website.

Catch your ideas by writing on this page.

Use a "Hook"

CRAFTING A STRONG TITLE

Use Keyword Phrases to Attract Readers

No matter what you have read over the past year or so about what works or does not work in search engine optimization, or what Google is or isn't doing to rate content to be sure people reach the information they want; you will shoot yourself in the foot if you don't use a title or subtitle with keyword phrases your ideal readers are using to find information about your particular subject.

Ebooks by SEO experts provide step by step instructions on how to find the best keyword phrases for your title. I recommend you check digital books rather than printed books because...*That's right, you already know*...an ebook has the most up to date information (check the publication and copyright dates to be sure).

As for me, I like to keep things simple. At the end of the day, the title needs to be factual, on point and short (easy to read when the book cover is the size of a postage stamp). It may not match a hot keyword phrase (but it can if you do a little research):

First, using Google's keywords tool, look for phrases that thousands of people use, and that have low competition.

Then, go into Amazon.com and type those phrases in the BOOKS search box. If those terms automatically self-populate Amazon's search box, you know a few people searched Amazon for that phrase. It won't report how many – could be a little, could be a lot – but someone besides you has been looking for that topic or title.

Catch your ideas by writing on this page.

This is the main reason I check Google first. The higher the number of searches there, the more likely proportional searches will be going on within the world of Amazon.

THE PERFECT TITLE

Coming up with a terrific title may take a little work. The original working title of A Writer's Guide to Fame and Fortune, was "The Expert Author." At the time, it said what I wanted it to say, was short and catchy; but guess what – "expert author" got zero results as a keyword phrase. Out it went.

Back to Google. "A writer's guide" netted 40,500, "fame and fortune" 74,000, and "time and money" 301,000. A double check in the Amazon Kindle search box and all phrases show up. Bingo. I have my title.

Now that we've explored keyword phrases, there are a few other factors to consider before deciding on the perfect title.

Online book buyers don't read – they scan.

The title shouldn't leave room for individual interpretation. You want your readers to know exactly what your book is about. "The Value of Childhood Dreams – Exploit your career aura to reach your potential" is a title that tells the reader... Well, it tells them nothing, actually. It's a terrible title. I normally wouldn't bother taking two minutes to check out the search terms in Google, but for you, I did (all were low on competition, so they did meet that criteria). Here's what came up:

"The value of" – 68,000,000 (lots of people searching for this, but the book wouldn't even make a showing in the Google ranks under this search term – most people never click past the first two or three pages)

Catch your ideas by writing on this page.

"Childhood dreams" – 12,100 (not bad, but – that's right – this book isn't about childhood dreams)

"Your career aura" – 0

"Reach your potential" – 3,600 (too low)

Remember:

- No more than four or five words for the main title (three words are better, two are ideal); but you can use however many are necessary for the sub-title (keyword phrases need to be in the sub-title).

- Check Google for high traffic, low competition (meaning that people who pay to advertise on Google are not using those terms, so your book won't have to compete with paid advertising)

- Check Amazon.com to see if those same keyword phrases are being searched

- Put as many relevant keyword phrases in your title and sub-title as possible

Catch your ideas by writing on this page.

Compose a Strong Author Bio

This is a fact. Not only are you the right person to write your book, you are the ONLY person who can. You know your subject cold, have a unique point of view, and have a passion to share what you've learned. Now write an author biography – or "bio" – that says just that. Don't be shy. This is no time for modesty.

"But what if I'm self taught?" In that case, briefly outline your journey beginning with how you first became interested in your subject, what you learned along the way, and how it led to writing a book. Keep in mind that the definition of an expert is "a person who has special skill or knowledge in some particular field; specialist." If you are skilled or knowledgeable in a particular activity or subject, you are an expert. Get used to the idea.

AMAZON'S AUTHOR CENTRAL

Look at the bios of other expert authors, whether in your related field or in others. They will give you ideas about what qualifies as part of an author's biography.

Join Amazon.com's Author Central for help writing your author bio. Author Central is an excellent resource in any case.

RESOURCES & RECOMMENDATIONS

Amazon Author Central – http://www.authorcentral.amazon.com

LinkedIn – http://www.linkedin.com

Catch your ideas by writing on this page.

Create a Killer Cover

MAKE IT "CLICKABLE"

Know what the good news is about most ebook covers? They are "gawd-awful." Why is that good news? Because yours will be professionally designed and look terrific; standing out like a white mouse at a black cat convention.

If you are a graphic designer, and are certain you can knock out a killer cover; have at it. If not, please hire a professional. The cover of your book is critical – you heard me right – *critical* to its success. A shoddy cover suggests that what is inside is shoddy as well. Don't be shoddy. Be sharp.

KNOW THE GROUND RULES

- The title must be easy to read even when the cover is very, very small (especially when selling online)

- The colors and background image needs to enhance the title, not overpower it.

- Everything should look great in black and white (nice contrast), as most eReaders don't "do color" – yet.

- Follow Amazon.com guidelines: Do not include unnecessary or confusing objects; extra text, graphics, or inset images; nor pornographic or offensive materials.

USE A PROFESSIONAL

After months of writing, you certainly don't want to bury your brilliance beneath a weak (or ugly) cover. Hire a professional.

Catch your ideas by writing on this page.

Go Digital

The most effective way to publish a book today (effective as in quick to market, successful promotion, and actual dollar sales) is to go digital first. Once actual book sales grow, add print on demand (POD) technology, or approach a traditional publishing house with solid facts and figures, including a full blown book proposal already proven successful.

Launch your book digitally, especially if you are a first-time author. Digital publishing allows you to upload your book, and see it online and available within a few days.

Digital publishing is the least expensive way to test how the market will react to your book. The format allows you to correct mistakes, and make timely updates. If the title is not working, change the cover, and resubmit.

HOW TO PUBLISH YOUR BOOK FOR THE KINDLE

Rather than presume to improve on Amazon's instructions, the following links will take you directly to their free guides.

Note: If you are serious about writing and publishing your book as an expert author, you will need to own a Kindle. In the meantime, if you don't have a Kindle, download the appropriate app to read Kindle books on your computer (PC or Mac).

- [How to] Build Your Book for Kindle / PC –
  http://amzn.to/T0maxx

- [Application] Use Kindle on Your PC Computer –
  http://www.amazon.com/kindleforpc

Catch your ideas by writing on this page.

- [How to] Build Your Book for Kindle / Mac – http://amzn.to/T0m8FZ

- [Application] Use Kindle on Your Mac Computer – http://www.amazon.com/kindleformac

HOW TO PUBLISH TO BARNES & NOBLES' PUBIT!

[And the Sony eReader]

Barnes & Noble / PubIt! – http://bit.ly/T0n7WK

Sony – http://ebookstore.sony.com/publishers/

RESOURCES & RECOMMENDATIONS

Build Your Book for Kindle / PC – http://amzn.to/T0maxx

Use Kindle on Your PC Computer – http://www.amazon.com/kindleforpc

Build Your Book for Kindle / Mac – http://amzn.to/T0m8FZ

Use Kindle on Your Mac Computer – http://www.amazon.com/kindleformac

Barnes & Noble / PubIt! – http://bit.ly/T0n7WK

Sony – http://ebookstore.sony.com/publishers/

Catch your ideas by writing on this page.

Work on Your Platform

Congratulations! You are a member of the elite 2% who actually write and produce a finished book. Exceptional. Take a few moments to focus on that accomplishment and savor how it feels. Good, yes? Give yourself a break for a day or two, then shore up your author platform.

Similar to the exposure you have when using a stage or podium to address a group of people, an author's platform allows you to increase your visibility, reach and influence in the market.

BUILDING AN AUTHOR PLATFORM

Most likely you have one started, because a platform is not a physical thing; it is a body of work. As an expert in your field of study, you probably have many of the platform materials below already in place; which is to your advantage.

A sturdy author platform includes:

- A website with an active blog
- Articles
- White papers
- Email newsletters
- Excerpts
- A social media network (Twitter, Facebook, LinkedIn)
- Podcasts, videos
- Digital downloads
- Speeches
- Collaborations

Catch your ideas by writing on this page.

EXPERT AUTHOR IN 20 STEPS

1. View yourself as a brand.

2. Think of yourself as an author.

3. Grasp the independent publishing opportunity.

4. Chose to publish your book yourself.

5. Take a look at the big picture.

6. Set goals and prepare to write.

7. Plan your book and use a notebook to capture your ideas.

8. Identify your ideal market.

9. Decide on your subject.

10. Meet your competition.

11. Take stock of everything you've done so far.

12. Get serious about writing.

13. Write your chapter outline first.

14. Write the first draft.

15. Edit for the critics who will read your book.

16. Pick a title with a strong "hook."

17. Compose your author bio.

18. Create a "clickable" cover.

19. Definitely go digital.

20. Consistently work on your platform.

Catch your ideas by writing on this page.

A LAST WORD.

Advances in technology have gifted the independent author/publisher with one of the greatest marketing opportunities since the advent of direct mail; the ability to publish their work themselves, and experience the many benefits of authorship, faster than ever before.

If you are a consultant, practitioner, entrepreneur, business professional, self employed, or have a unique combination of experience and expertise to share, seriously consider taking advantage of the self publishing revolution. I believe it is the fastest way to grow your business and get the respect you deserve, the work you want, and the money you're worth.

Amy Lorenti – July 14, 2012

Look for these new Kindle titles from Amy Lorenti in September 2012 at Amazon.com:

A Business Plan for Savvy Writers

A Marketing Plan for Savvy Writers

A Promotion Plan for Savvy Writers

ABOUT THE AUTHOR

AMY LORENTI – author, graphic designer, editor, public relations and marketing consultant – built two graphic design and corporate communication agencies in the New York metro area during the '80s and '90s working primarily for Fortune 500 companies headquartered up and down the I-95 corridor. After relocating to the Research Triangle region of North Carolina she founded klearIDEA to focus on serving the needs of the small business owners. Ms. Lorenti works with small businesses, entrepreneurs, independents, and professionals to help them take advantage of today's online opportunities while establishing a professional online presence for their companies, and a strong personal brand. She works closely with subject matter experts to help them write, publish, and promote their books.

Amy lives in North Carolina with her son and their two cats. Besides her client work, she is preparing another book for aspiring authors; and is writing a murder mystery; both scheduled for release in the fall of 2012.

CONTACT INFORMATION

PR, Marketing & Ghostwriting Services: *amy@klearIDEA.com*

Speaking Engagements & Author Workshops: *amy@lorentiWRITES.com*

Blog: *http://www.amylorenti.com*

Author site: *http://www.lorentiWRITES.com*

LinkedIn: *http://www.linkedin.com/in/lorenti*

Twitter: *http://twitter.com/#!/amylorenti*

Facebook Fan Page: *http://www.facebook.com/pages/Lorenti-Writes/181587785239243*